21ST Century Skills INNOVATION LIBRARY | Design a Better World

A Better App

Heather Newman

Published in the United States of America by Cherry Lake Publishing
Ann Arbor, Michigan
www.cherrylakepublishing.com

Content Adviser: Kristin Fontichiaro, University of Michigan School of Information, Ann Arbor, MI
Reading Adviser: Marla Conn MS, Ed., Literacy specialist, Read-Ability, Inc.

Photo Credits: © LightField Studios/Shutterstock.com, cover, 1, 5; © Beer5020/Shutterstock.com, 6; © Sam Bateman/Shutterstock.com, 9; © Myimagine/Shutterstock.com, 11; © Pressmaster/Shutterstock.com, 15; © FOXARTBOX/Shutterstock.com, 17; © Michelle Baumbach/Shutterstock.com, 19; © Chaosamran_Studio/Shutterstock.com, 23; © FirmBee/pixabay.com, 25; © Rei Imagine/Shutterstock.com, 29

Graphic Element Credits: © Ohn Mar/Shutterstock.com, back cover, multiple interior pages; © Dmitrieva Katerina/Shutterstock.com, back cover, multiple interior pages; © advent/Shutterstock.com, back cover, front cover, multiple interior pages; © Visual Generation/Shutterstock.com, multiple interior pages; © anfisa focusova/Shutterstock.com, front cover, multiple interior pages; © Babich Alexander/Shutterstock.com, back cover, front cover, multiple interior pages

Library of Congress Cataloging-in-Publication Data

Names: Newman, Heather, 1970- author.
Title: A better app / by Heather Newman.
Description: Ann Arbor : Cherry Lake Publishing, [2019] | Series: Design a better world | Includes bibliographical references and index. | Audience: Grade 4 to 6.
Identifiers: LCCN 2018039434| ISBN 9781534143234 (hardcover) | ISBN 9781534139794 (pbk.) | ISBN 9781534140998 (pdf) | ISBN 9781534142190 (hosted ebook)
Subjects: LCSH: Mobile apps–Juvenile literature. | Application software–Development–Juvenile literature. | Smartphones–Programming–Juvenile literature.
Classification: LCC QA76.59 .N49 2019 | DDC 005.35–dc23
LC record available at https://lccn.loc.gov/2018039434

Printed in the United States of America
Corporate Graphics

Table of Contents

CHAPTER ONE

Design Thinking and Identifying a Problem

Have you ever played a video game and wished the controls worked differently? Or tried to send someone a message and had it not turn out the way you expected, with mistakes in the text or with the emojis? If you've ever looked at something—especially using technology—and thought, "This could work even better," you've found a good **design problem**.

A design problem happens anytime something doesn't work as well as it should. Almost every design problem can be solved, and all it takes is someone like you to see what's wrong and decide to fix it! One of the best ways to figure out how to solve design problems is to use a process called **design thinking**. A company called IDEO put design thinking on the map. Design thinking is a way of looking at problems and figuring out solutions that work for a bunch of different people. It can be used to solve all kinds of problems. In this book, you'll learn how to use design thinking to build a better app, step by step.

To start, you'll want to break down how an app works. Each app has a bunch of different parts to consider. Ask yourself:

- How do you pick what you want to do? Do you use buttons, swipe an area of the screen, or choose from one of those horizontal "hamburger" menus?

Design thinking can help you improve the things you use every day—like your backpack or the school bus.

Thinking about the ways you use your own apps can help you identify a problem to investigate.

- Do the apps you like use the phone's camera or sensors such as the one that detects whether the phone is vertical or horizontal?
- Do they let you type things in, or are you always selecting or swiping instead?
- Once you've selected something or typed something in, does the app do the action right away? Or do you have to confirm what you wanted?

Apps have two parts. One is the functionality, which is what the app can do for you. The other is the UI, short for "user interface," which is how the app shows you things on-screen and lets you pick what you want to happen. You'll want to think about both parts when you design your app.

Try This

Pull up your favorite app on a mobile phone and look at it closely. What do you use it for? What does it need from you—button pushes, information, lines you draw with your fingertip? What do you get out of it? This is the functionality of the app.

Now look at how the screen itself is laid out. Where are the graphics, buttons, boxes, text, or other pieces placed on the screen? Do you type or swipe or tap? How do things look when you use them? Are they easy to use? This is the user interface, or UI.

Consider your favorite app: What do you like about its functionality? What do you need it to do, and does it do that function well? How about the UI? Do the app's screens make it easy to figure out what to do? Are the buttons big enough to tap? Is the text big enough to read in sunlight? Is the next step you need to take bright and clear on the screen? Now repeat this with an app that doesn't feel useful to you.

Make a list of things you like and things that could be better. These are the possible design problems, and you'll use this list in Chapter 2.

CHAPTER TWO

Research, Observe, and Interview

Chapter 1 should have given you some ideas about ways that an app could be better. Now you'll collect more information to figure out what you want to build into your own app. You'll use three techniques: research, **observation**, and interviews. This is super fun, because you get to talk to other people about their suggestions and ideas—and everyone likes to talk about those!

Bring a notebook to write down some short phrases to remind you about what people said. Or print out a screenshot of an app, and then draw or write on the printout! As you collect information, think about answering two questions: What problem is your app trying to solve? And how do other people solve that problem right now, with or without an app?

Research

Start by watching other people to see how they solve the problem your app will tackle. If you're trying to build a better calendar app, look at how people use calendars in everyday life. Does your family have a wall

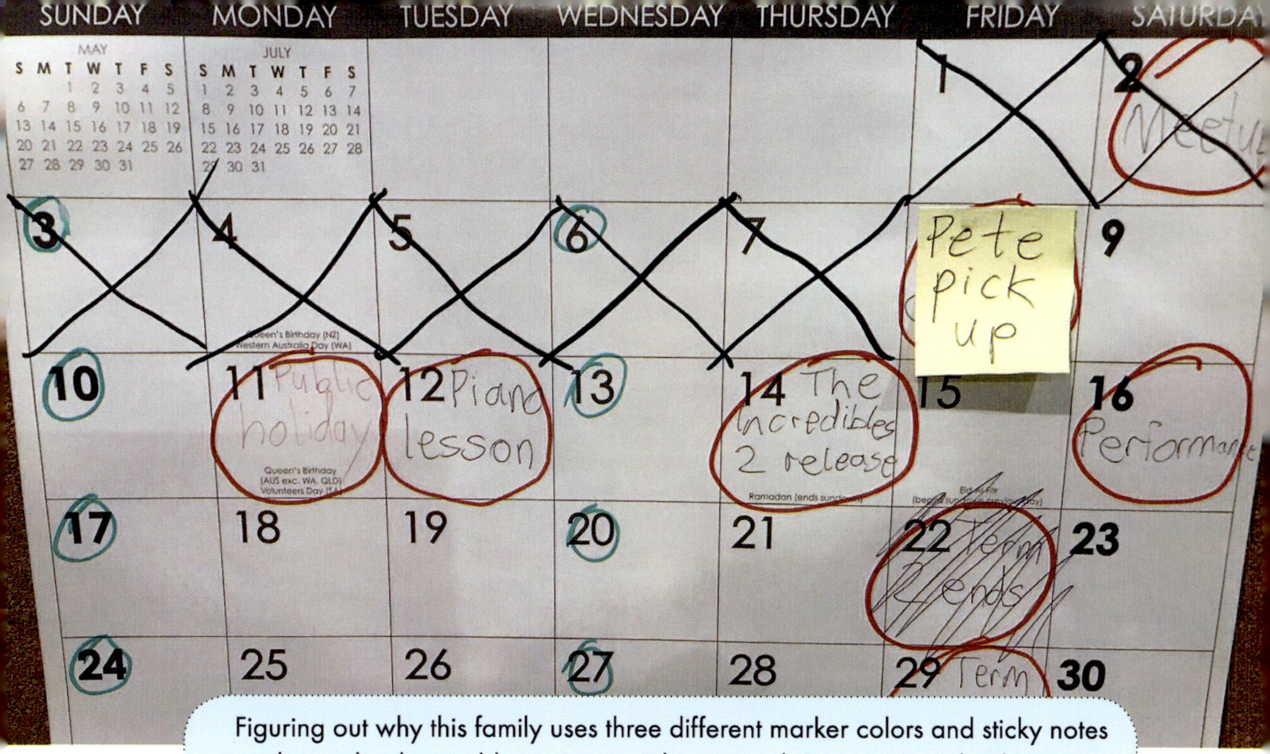

Figuring out why this family uses three different marker colors and sticky notes on their calendar could give you insight as you design a new calendar app.

calendar to keep track of activities and vacations? Do your teachers use calendars in the classroom to help you keep up on lessons, tests, and homework?

Then look at apps like the one you want to build. You can go to the Apple App Store or Google Play store and search for keywords. Think about what the app is for and what it does. These are the words you should type into the search box to find out what other apps are out there.

Once you find some, look at the screenshots to see what they do (the functionality) and what they look like or how they behave (the UI). Do you like the colors? Do you like the way they work or how they make you feel? Make a list of what you like and don't like, and what design elements, **features**, and **interactivity** the apps seem to use often. Consider all those aspects you read about in Chapter 1.

Observe

Now, watch people using apps. If they don't already have an app similar to the problem you're studying, show them the best one you found when you were doing your research. Ask them to try it out. Make a list of some of the things you'd want your app to do, and ask them to try to do those things with their app.

For instance, if it's a calendar app, you could ask them to make a new appointment, then change the time, then delete the appointment. Ask everyone to do the same things, so you can see how different people approach the same task.

This is kind of like being a spy. You don't want to tell someone *how* to do what you've asked. That's cheating! To give you the best information, they should figure it out by themselves. You just want to take notes as they use the app. Ask them to talk out loud about what they're doing, sort of like a narrator in a story.

- What are they typing or tapping on?
- What do they think is happening?
- What do they like and not like about the app as they use it?
- Are things confusing or clear?
- Do they get the results they want, or do they want more features?

Make notes in your notebook or on the screenshot printouts. Draw green circles around things that work great and red ones around things that need work. Draw arrows to point to specific parts of the screen.

Watch how friends and family use their apps to learn how users respond to different kinds of app functions.

Interview

Getting someone's ideas about an app that already exists is great. But you also want to know how they *want* to use that app and what problem they're trying to solve with it. Write down a list of questions, and ask family, friends, and teachers the same ones.

- What things do they think the app will make easier?
- How will such an app make their lives better?
- In an ideal world, what would they want the app to do for them?
- What kinds of situations would they use it in? If they're going to use it outdoors or in a store, they'll probably want it to look and act differently than if they're using it quietly indoors on their couch.

Try This

1. **Research:** Search the App Store or Google Play store for apps like yours or made for people like you. Check the reviews for those apps—they can help you know what people appreciate or dislike about various existing solutions. Make a list of the features you like, such as colors, how it looks, how it works, and how it feels. What don't you like? What would you do better?
2. **Observe:** Ask some potential users of your app to let you watch while they use their favorite apps on their phones. Ask them to narrate, or talk through, what they are thinking about as they use the app. This will give you insights into why they are interacting with the app the way they are.
3. **Interview:** Talk with at least two people who might be potential users of an app like yours. Also talk to one person who IDEO would call an "extreme user"—someone who especially needs the app or already uses one like it a lot. For example, a lawyer who bills by the fraction of the hour may use their calendar app hundreds of times a day to keep track of each tiny task—that's extreme! Try and talk with other people who might use your app that are different than you. If you're a girl, talk to boys, and vice versa. What about people who are older or younger than you? What do they want from this kind of app?

CHAPTER THREE

Synthesize and Focus

By now, you've got a lot of notes. It's time to put them all together—with friends!

Synthesizing

Synthesizing is the process of listening for **themes** in your collection of notes. Was there one particular thing that many people said they wanted to be able to do? What did you see them frequently get frustrated by?

Gather all your notes and printouts, and grab some friends to help. The more ideas you hear from your design team, the more useful your app will be to lots of people. Together, look over what people said and make a list of the problems they had—with the apps as well as with the issue your app hopes to solve. For instance, if you're working on a calendar app, a list of other people's thoughts might include:

- Too easy to forget what's going on tomorrow
- Too little space to write down what an appointment is for
- No good place to include things that are due that day
- Need more reminders for tasks, not just appointments

Once you've synthesized your notes, choose one problem to focus on.

- Reminder alarms are difficult to set or hear
- Changing an appointment requires lots of taps and typing
- Screen is hard to read in sunlight
- App is too noisy in the classroom or library

Focusing

Now you have a list of problems that your app will try to solve. You want to pick just one to **focus** on. Pick one that's important to you or your team or that a lot of people talked about. You might choose one that you think you will have good ideas to solve.

Check out other apps available to be sure you're not attempting to solve a problem that's already been solved!

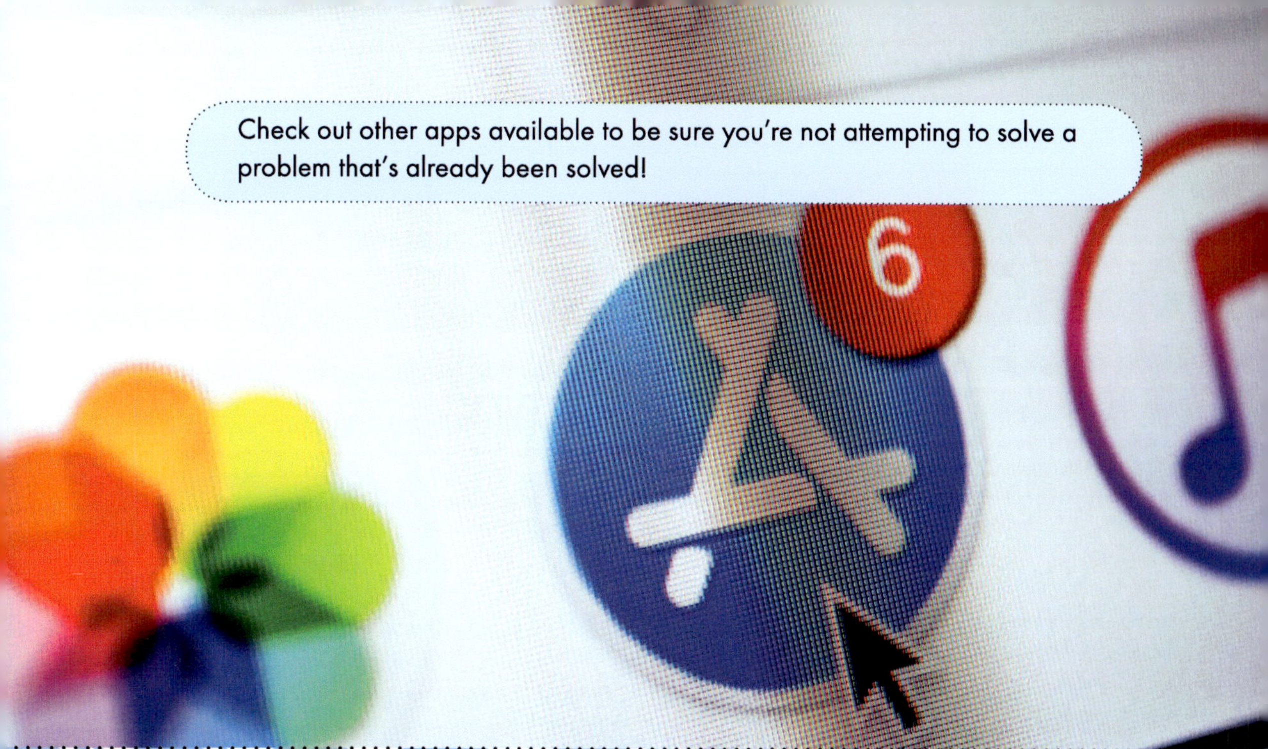

Try This

Get your design team and make a list of problems you could solve, based on all your notes. Try writing everything out on a whiteboard so the whole team can see. Figure out what one issue you'll tackle first. You'll use these in Chapter 4!

CHAPTER FOUR

Brainstorm

Now you know what problem your app will try to solve. It's time to come up with all kinds of ideas for how to solve it. That's called **brainstorming**. You're not trying to figure out which ideas to use yet—this is all about how many ideas you have, not which ones are best.

Here is one way to jump-start your thinking. Say to yourself, "To solve ________, we will design and test ________." For instance, let's take the problem of the calendar app being too noisy in the classroom or library. You might say:

To solve calendar apps that make too much noise at school, we will design and test:

- Quieter or more pleasant alert sounds
- Using the phone's location information to automatically make it silent in some places
- Automatically skipping all alerts at certain times of the day
- Displaying a message on-screen instead
- Alerts that sound only through headphones
- Using the flashing light on the phone
- A special phone case that will change color when an alert is happening

Loud calendar alerts can cause problems in class. How might you fix this problem?

- An app that messages a friend who can wave at you when you need to go
- Making the phone vibrate
- Automatically making alerts silent or quieter if your phone is facedown
- Making alerts that keep the phone screen lit up longer so you'll see them
- Making the phone release a scent so you can smell it instead
- Asking people whether they want an alert at all when they put something on the calendar

Did you notice? Some of these ideas are about things the app could do. But others address new ways people can use the app. Brainstorming will bring out your solutions even when they're not obvious. That's why it's important to write every idea down, no matter how wacky it seems.

Try This

Try using these two brainstorming techniques: the mind map and the "Yes, and . . ." mind-set.

The Mind Map

One method for brainstorming by yourself, especially if you get stuck for new ideas, is to use a mind map. This is a drawing that helps you think of new ideas that are related to one another.

Grab a piece of poster board and a pencil, and put the problem statement in the center: "To solve ________, we will design and test ________." Now draw a circle around it. This is the center of your mind map.

Draw a bunch of lines leading out from the center, and put a circle at the end of each line. These are for ideas related to the problem. For our calendar app, you might use a circle for each of the ways you can think of that people might get alerts: sounds, lights, the screen, smells, buzzing, or things they can feel, you name it.

Now draw lines out from each of those circles. On those lines, start to list all the ideas you can think of that relate to each of those concepts. So for lights, it might be lights that flash, lights that change color, lights that gradually get brighter or dimmer, or lights that move.

If you find that you have lots of ideas that seem to group together, you can always make another circle at the end of *those* lines and keep going. This is why doing a mind map in pencil can be useful—so you can erase or make new circles when you want to! Don't be afraid to draw pictures or use colors.

Yes, And . . .

Comedians do a type of comedy called improvisation where they have to make up funny things on the spot. They invented the "Yes, and . . ." technique as a way to build on each other's jokes! Now many companies and organizations use it for brainstorming.

For your group brainstorming, gather your friends and get a big piece of poster board. Across the top of it, write your problem statement: "To solve ________, we will design and test ________."

Ask someone to mention any idea at all. Write it down. Now ask another person to come up with an idea. The only rule is that they have to start *their* idea with "Yes, and . . ."

So to use our example, the first person might say, "We should make a phone case that changes color when an alert comes in." The second person might say, "Yes, and you could change the colors so they matched your backpack." The third might say, "Yes, and the app should use the same colors for its on-screen alerts." The fourth might say, "Yes, and we should also make an on-screen message."

People can change ideas whenever they like, proposing wild new things or building on the previous idea. Brainstorming this way means that everyone gets a turn to suggest an idea—even your quiet friends—and that they feel like the person after them heard what they had to say.

CHAPTER FIVE

Prototype

You should have a big list of some pretty great ideas. It's time to pick one or more to try. You'll want to start by building a **prototype**. This is a quick, easy sample of the solution you want to try out. For your prototype, try drawing what you think your app should look like with a pencil on paper.

Some people want to jump right into coding their app the moment they have an idea. But you'll get where you're going faster if you make prototypes like this instead. Pencil drawings are a lot easier to change than computer code!

When you draw your app, don't forget to include both the functionality and the UI: what it will do and how it will look. Things like where buttons are located or how people will tell the app what to do are important. For example, how easy will it be for your friends to reach that button with their thumbs? Your prototype will help them to imagine it.

The more detailed your prototype is, the easier it will be to code your app.

Try This

Sketch out five versions of what your app could look like with pencil and paper. Use a pencil so you can easily make changes later or colored markers to help you see the different features!

CHAPTER SIX

Test, Adjust, Test Again

Now that you've got your prototypes in hand, it's time to figure out whether they work. The best people to help you find that out are the ones you talked with originally who had the problem and needed a solution. In design thinking (and when you're building an app!), these people are called users, because they use your product or idea.

Testing Your App with Users

Take the ideas you sketched out during the prototype process and show them to three people. Try to avoid giving any reasons for why you did things—you don't want to make them think about your app in any particular way.

Listening to Feedback

Getting feedback on your work can be tough. For example, someone might say, "I don't like the colors you used in your app." It's important to avoid getting defensive or arguing. Your job right now is to listen. You can decide later whether to make a change, especially if a lot of other people say the same thing.

You might be surprised about what users have to say about your prototype.

You can ask questions to help them make their thoughts more specific. You might ask a follow-up question like, "What about the colors bugs you?" They might answer, "Having the black writing on a dark-blue background like this makes it really hard to read." Bingo! That's a problem you can understand and fix.

Asking follow-up questions makes the feedback you get more helpful and lets the person you're talking to know you're listening to what they are saying. Don't forget to take notes!

Reviewing Feedback

Once you've collected all your notes with people's comments about your app, look them over for themes and ideas. This is a lot like the *synthesize and focus* steps earlier—you can even use the same group of friends! Decide which problems are the most urgent. What do people like best about your app? Can you include even more of those features? What do people like least that you might change or remove?

Adjust and Test Again

Use the advice you've decided would be useful, and make those tweaks on your prototypes. This is why you drew them in pencil—so that it would be easy to make changes to your design. Now go back to those people, or to others, and get their feedback again!

Try This

Take the five sketches from the last chapter, and ask these questions. Keep count of people's answers:

- Does this app do what you need it to do? Why or why not?
- What is your favorite part of this app?
- If you were going to change or improve something, what would it be?
- What would make this app easier to use?
- What would make this app more fun to look at?

CHAPTER SEVEN

Implement!

You've gotten a lot of feedback and made a lot of tweaks—you're finally ready to build your app! Coding apps is a lot of fun. Typically, what you're doing is drawing the elements on-screen that you want, then telling the app what you want those things to do. Different websites can help you create your app.

One site to consider is Thunkable (www.thunkable.com). It lets you drag and drop different UI elements (boxes to type in, buttons to click, text to read) right onto the screen. Drop-down menus let you choose what each item will do after someone uses it. You can create Apple and Android apps with this tool.

Another site to try is App Inventor, which Google originally made and the people at the Massachusetts Institute of Technology now keep up-to-date (http://appinventor.mit.edu). App Inventor creates Android apps only.

Whenever you're using new services like these, look for pages at the site that will help you learn. Find the section labeled "Tutorial." Just like a tutorial in a video game, these videos or instructions will walk you through what you need to know to build your app on the site!
You can also search for the name of the site and "tutorial" on YouTube.

Creating apps that make life easier for people can be rewarding!

Now you're done building a better app! If you really want to put design thinking to the test, you'll continue to show your app to people, get their feedback, and tweak the app. Making small changes over and over—called iterating—will help you come up with the very best solution to a problem.

Learn More

Books

Cook, Eric. *Prototyping*. Ann Arbor, MI: Cherry Lake Publishing, 2015.

Fontichiaro, Kristin. *Design Thinking*. Ann Arbor, MI: Cherry Lake Publishing, 2015.

Van Lent, Colleen. *Web Design with HTML5*. Ann Arbor, MI: Cherry Lake Publishing, 2015.

Websites

YouTube—IDEO Shopping Cart Project
https://youtu.be/W6EgoiPxNDs
Many Americans first learned about IDEO from this television profile.

The Nueva School—Design Thinking and Engineering at Nueva
www.nuevaschool.org/academics/design-thinking
Learn how one school incorporates design thinking into its programs.

Glossary

brainstorming (BRAYN-storm-ing) thinking of as many ideas as possible

design problem (dih-ZINE PRAH-bluhm) something that doesn't work well that you think you can make better can

design thinking (dih-ZINE THINGK-ing) a process for studying, testing, and solving problems

features (FEE-churz) things that are unique or special about a product or service

focus (FOH-kuhs) to narrow down to one idea or really concentrate on one thing

interactivity (IN-tur-ack-tuv-uh-tee) the two-way communication between an electronic system and human user

observation (ahb-zur-VAY-shuhn) the act of looking closely at something

prototype (PROH-tuh-tipe) a "first draft" of an invention

synthesizing (SIN-thuh-size-ing) looking at a lot of ideas and figuring out what the big picture is or what the patterns are

themes (THEEMZ) ideas or concepts that appear over and over

Index

Heather Newman has written hundreds of stories and books about technology over more than 25 years. She works for the University of Michigan School of Information, where students use design thinking every day!